THE JESUS I WISH I KNEW IN HIGH SCHOOL

Asian American Edition

Edited by
Kevin Yi, Rooted Ministry

New Growth Press, Greensboro, NC 27401
newgrowthpress.com

Cover Design: Dan Stelzer
Interior Typesetting and eBook: Lisa Parnell, lparnellbookservices.com
Series Editor: Cameron Cole

ISBN: 978-1-64507-456-4 (paperback)
ISBN: 978-1-64507-457-1 (ebook)

Library of Congress Cataloging-in-Publication Data
Names: Yi, Kevin, 1981– editor.
Title: The Jesus I wish I knew in high school / edited by Kevin Yi, Rooted Ministry.
Other titles: Jesus I wish I knew in high school (Asian American edition)
Description: Asian American edition. | Greensboro, NC : New Growth Press, [2024] | Asian American edition of: The Jesus I wish I knew in high school / edited by Cameron Cole and Charlotte Getz. Greensboro, NC : New Growth Press, [2021] | Audience: Ages 14-18 | Audience: Grades 10-12
Identifiers: LCCN 2024013911 (print) | LCCN 2024013912 (ebook) | ISBN 9781645074564 (paperback) | ISBN 9781645074571 (ebook)
Subjects: LCSH: Asian American Christians—Religious life—Juvenile literature. | Asian American Christians—Race identity—Juvenile literature. | Christian teenagers—Religious life—Juvenile literature.
Classification: LCC BR563.A82 J47 2024 (print) | LCC BR563.A82 (ebook) | DDC 248.8/3—dc23/eng/20240531
LC record available at https://lccn.loc.gov/2024013911
LC ebook record available at https://lccn.loc.gov/2024013912

Printed in the United States of America

31 30 29 28 27 26 25 24 3 4 5 6

Contents

Foreword v
by Cameron Cole

Introduction 1
by Clark Fobes IV

Chapter 1: Performance Pressure and the Finished Work of Christ 5
by Danny Kwon, PhD

Chapter 2: Unworthiness and the God Who Saves 10
by Connie Leung Nelson

Chapter 3: Weakness and the God of Strength 15
by Ashley Kim

Chapter 4: Church Hurt and the Good Shepherd 20
by Justin Wong

Chapter 5: Cultural Confusion and Identity in Christ 25
by Cory Ishida

Chapter 6: Tragedy and a Better Friend 30
by Daniel Yang

Chapter 7: Trying to Fit In and God's Acceptance 36
by E. L. Sherene Joseph

Chapter 8: Breaking the Rules and the God Who Forgives.... 41
by Terrence Shay

Chapter 9: Loneliness and the God Who Is Near 46
by Soojin Park

Chapter 10: Masculinity and the Son of Man 51
by Felix Theonugraha, PhD

Chapter 11: Multiethnicity and the Family of God 57
by Raymond Chang

Chapter 12: Feeling Forgotten and God's Adoption 63
by Jonathan Holmes

Afterword 69
by Kevin Yi

Glossary 71

Foreword

by Cameron Cole

Several years ago, I had the privilege of preaching in the English service of a Korean American immigrant church in Los Angeles. I told the story of being a young person living under immense pressure. My life had centered around excelling in every area, with the end target being acceptance into a top-flight college.

I worked constantly, with no breaks, thinking that I had to prove my worth by getting the best grades, managing loads of extracurricular and service opportunities, and being a model of success in every endeavor.

My religious experience largely poured gas on that fire. Some well-meaning Christians in my life had taught me that a life of devotion to God involved optimal performance. According to these mentors, once I gained salvation, the Lord expected me to give maximal effort to being the best Christian possible for God's glory. What I heard was that God's grace and mercy only relevant to my salvation but had no bearing on my day-to-day experience of the Christian life.

This miserable, performance-based life led me to a colossal crash and burn after college. I finally had to admit that I couldn't do it all and that I was not thriving in any area of life, much less in my relationship with God. My life changed and healing began when I heard these freeing words: *The gospel is rest. The gospel means Jesus carries the burden of your life. The gospel means you'll never have to prove yourself again. You are loved apart from your performance.*

When I shared this story at the Korean American church, I noticed tears starting to stream down the faces of many in the audience. I had enough cultural knowledge from my Asian American friends to realize that such a public outpouring of emotion was unique in this setting.

After the sermon, I asked my friends, Kevin and Tracy Yi, about what had just happened. Why was everyone crying? Kevin said, "You just told their story."

Maybe you are experiencing similar performance pressures at this stage of your life. On top of that, you may be experiencing additional challenges related to being part of a minority culture. Although I have not experienced everything you are experiencing, I do know it's hard—really, really, hard—to be a teenager, no matter your life's circumstances. Adolescence inherently involves loneliness, pressure, anxiety, self-doubt, fears, temptations, and failures. It is the prayer of the Rooted Ministry team that you will find the following devotions particularly encouraging for the unique challenges you are facing. We want you to know that a group of adults recognizes how hard and demanding this life stage is for you right now. We want you to feel seen and understood.

All of the writers in this book come from Asian American backgrounds. They know the particular challenges and blessings that you are facing as an Asian American person. We want you to see and appreciate God's glory in your ethnic heritage.

Finally, we want you to see how Jesus and his glorious gospel can give you the hope and strength to flourish—not just survive—these years. We want you to feel the comfort and healing that the congregation at the Korean American church felt when they were reminded that God loves us apart from our performance. On your best days and your worst days, God's deep affection for you remains the same because of the life, death, and resurrection of Jesus.

You're going to make it, because Christ is with you and for you.

Introduction

by Clark Fobes IV

As a half-Korean, half-White kid growing up in San Francisco, I never quite felt like I fit in. This is not a unique feeling for those going through their adolescent years. Whether due to personality, style, or interests, many teenagers recount feelings of social loneliness. The loneliness I felt, however, stemmed from a more fundamental characteristic: my ethnicity and race.

I grew up in a predominantly Black neighborhood, so I often felt like an outsider on my own block. While there were plenty of Asians living in San Francisco, there were hardly any Koreans, let alone mixed-race Asians. I found myself as the lone White-faced kid among my Chinese friends. I always felt different from my White friends because of my Asian heritage and culture. I never felt Asian enough to be accepted by my Asian friends, but I never felt American enough to belong with my White friends.

This struggle to find one's cultural and social belonging is shared by most Asians living outside of their countries of heritage. Some have described this experience as feeling like a foreigner in one's own land.

In answer to this search for belonging, our world has encouraged us to carve out a path for ourselves. We've been told to demand our belonging if no one will give it to us, and to advocate for greater representation. While these may be helpful and good at times, they are not the way Scripture calls us to answer this question: Where do we belong in this world?

In his letter to believers scattered throughout the Roman Empire, Peter answers this question by calling Christians to embrace their foreignness: "Beloved, I urge you as sojourners and exiles to abstain from the passions of the flesh, which wage war against your soul" (1 Peter 2:11). Rather than giving in to worldly desires and pursuits, Peter reminds us that the foreignness we feel is precisely what we *should* feel.

If Christians belong to another world, then we should never feel at home here in this one. As Russell Jeung—chair of Asian American Studies at San Francisco State University and cofounder of Stop AAPI Hate—says, "We shouldn't want to feel like we belong, because once we do, we've lost the sense of what makes us different in this world as Christians."[1]

According to Peter, our feeling of foreignness is not an obstacle to belonging in the world; it is an advantage to belonging in Christ. And the more we find ourselves in Christ, who himself was alienated among his own creation, the more we will experience the power of the gospel to live as exiles in a foreign land.

Even still, our experience of perpetual foreignness can tire and discourage us. Our desire for human belonging is fundamental to God's creating us. This desire has largely resulted in greater representation of Asians in public spaces. The recent successes of Asians in media are a testament to this—from TV and film to the global phenomenon of the K-pop craze.

The need for greater representation is largely what spurred on this book too. Kevin and I have often reflected together on our own experiences as Asian Americans. We've realized that while Asian stories are being told on large secular platforms, we've only just begun to tell them within Christian circles. Rooted's

1. Russell Jeung, "Stand for AAPI Lives and Dignity" (speech, National Rally for AAPI Lives and Dignity, Civic Center Plaza, San Francisco, CA, March 28, 2021).

first book in this series, *The Jesus I Wish I Knew in High School*, was beautifully diverse, but we felt there were more stories to be told from our uniquely Asian perspectives.

Most likely you picked this book up because you are an Asian American teenager looking for help to identify, understand, and process your own story in light of God's image and Christ's redemption. Our hope is that through each individual's story, you will see Asian American experiences lifted up with dignity and celebrated for their uniqueness. But we also hope that you will see yourself in them. As you read, we hope you will find both representation and a sense of belonging with these brothers and sisters, who are walking faithfully with Jesus in all of their ethnic and cultural distinctions.

Maybe you're reading this book as a parent of an Asian American teenager (whether you are Asian American, Asian immigrant, or even non-Asian yourself) to better understand the story of your child and how you can minister to him or her in light of the gospel. Or maybe you are simply a brother or sister in Christ seeking to understand the stories and experiences of your Asian friends. Our hope is that this book will help you better love and encourage the Asian American teenagers in your life as they seek to follow Jesus with their whole selves.

As I look back on my ethnically confused teenage self, I often wonder how my own journey might have been different if I'd had a book like this. I'm sure a lot of pain and emotional toil could have been prevented by just knowing I was seen—that there were other people experiencing the same things I was. Maybe I would have felt a greater sense of belonging in a world that rarely allowed me to belong, let alone validated my existence as a mixed-race person. But in hindsight, I'm grateful for the pain and isolation that became so characteristic of my story. Were it not for my feeling of alienation in the world, I may never have found the need to pursue Christ and to look for belonging with him and his people as Peter exhorts us.

When I think about my two daughters, who are three-quarters Korean, one-quarter White, my heart often breaks thinking about the struggles they will have to endure that I once did. I want to raise them in a world that will accept them fully for who they are, ethnically and culturally, celebrating all their differences and uniqueness. But I also know that as long as we are on this side of heaven, there will always be pain, brokenness, and the sins of racism, ignorance, prejudice, and pride. So my ultimate hope is not that they would find their belonging and comfort in the present world. My ultimate hope is that they would find their belonging and comfort in the God who created them in all their uniqueness, and who is in the process of redeeming every part of who they are. That's my desire for you, too, as you read this book.

You may never find the belonging you are hoping for among your friends or even within your own family or particular Asian community. You may never even feel fully at ease with who you are as an Asian American. Our greatest hope for you is not that you would find belonging in this world. Instead, we pray that any feeling of foreignness would cause you to cling closely to Christ and to the identity you have in him as a child of God and a citizen of his kingdom.

Chapter 1
Performance Pressure and the Finished Work of Christ
by Danny Kwon, PhD

My high school classmates repeatedly signed my yearbook, "Don't forget me when you are rich and famous," because that was my goal as I graduated from high school. As a teenager, I longed for a life of affluence and dreamed of becoming someone significant. I idolized movie characters and celebrities with lavish lives.

Hanging over much of my life was a nagging pressure to be successful. My parents worked sixteen-hour days running a dry cleaning business. Seeing my parents labor so hard as marginalized immigrants in America was deeply impactful. As I watched their hot, sweaty work, I turned their perseverance into a personal craving to be successful and even famous. I don't blame my parents or upbringing for this, but these expectations to succeed cast a shadow over all that I did.

This desire for significance also had roots in my childhood, as I experienced the honor-and-shame culture of an Asian American family. I was considered chubby, so my mother sometimes compared me with thinner kids and subtly suggested I lose weight. While her comments were not malicious in any way, the expectation to look presentable to others permeated my life as a young boy. Similarly, when one of my friends was excelling in baseball, my father began practicing with me every evening. I appreciated the time he spent with me despite his long work hours. But I also remember the expectations he placed on me to be just as good as my friend. I did not want to fail my father.

Then, as a teenager, there were the SATs, which were a nightmare. The score you received seemed like it would determine your whole future. After we received our test results in the mail (yes, they used to be mailed to us), there was always an awkward moment when classmates would ask for your score. It was easy to measure your worth against another student's SATs. There was this unspoken pressure to fib about your score by a few points to make yourself look better.

When the time came for me to apply to college, I pinned my hopes to the expectation of getting into an Ivy League school. I thought if only I could get into *one* prestigious university, all the pressure I felt would be relieved. Unfortunately, I got rejected by all the Ivy League schools to which I applied. I attended a good college with a full scholarship, but it still wasn't one of the Ivy League universities. I felt I had failed everyone, especially my parents. That sense of failure would continue to haunt me throughout my college years and beyond.

I avoided coming home from college for two full years because I felt my life did not measure up to the standards I had set for myself. While my parents were unconditionally loving and supportive, I lived under the weight of my perceived failures. I couldn't face my parents or my friends. In my deep sense of shame and embarrassment, I not only missed opportunities to be with my family; I also lost interest in going to church because I felt I had nothing to contribute. I lacked meaning and purpose, and life seemed without hope.

The Jesus I Wish I Knew

One day during the spring of my sophomore year, a friend in the dormitory invited me to a campus small group meeting. At this gathering, which I hadn't wanted to attend, God reminded me of the truth found in Ephesians 2:10. The apostle Paul writes, "For we are God's handiwork, created in Christ Jesus to do good works, which God prepared in advance for us to do" (NIV).

God used that small group to remind me of the gospel: that Jesus Christ's life, death, and resurrection had freed me from the expectations to perform or be successful. Because Jesus had taken my place, dying on the cross for my sin, I no longer had to measure up to some standard. The only standard that mattered was Jesus's perfect life in place of mine. This was all God's grace, and nothing I could boast about (Ephesians 2:9). In the words of Paul, my identity was now as God's "handiwork," a word that can also be translated as *masterpiece*.

I came to understand that I was no longer defined by the college I attended, my SAT score, how well I played baseball, or how much I weighed. Because of the love of Christ demonstrated on the cross and the power of his resurrection, my life was defined by Jesus—not by my success or failure.

Ephesians 2:10 also showed me that in Jesus Christ, God had a purpose for me. He had prepared "in advance" for me to do his good works. This reality freed me from the false notion that my success or lack thereof defined me.

As I took all this to heart, success and material riches ceased to be the driving force in my life. Rather, I felt liberated knowing that in Christ, God had good plans for me. I no longer felt the same weight of expectation in regard to my performance. God held my future, and I could find peace in him.

Looking back now to my high school days, I wish I had been able to speak the gospel to myself. I wish I could have heard Jesus saying to me, "You are not defined by your looks, your future success, or how other people might perceive you, but by *my* work in your place." Likewise, I wish I had been able to see then that God already had my future "prepared in advance." Rather than being driven by the unhealthy desire to become successful on the one hand, or by the toxic fear of failure on the other, I would have been able to place my future in the hope Jesus secured for me.

The Jesus I Want You to Know

You may be hoping to get into an Ivy League school like I was. You may be feeling that you need to become the most successful or wealthy student in your friend group.

You might be driven by a desire to be successful or renowned. Our social media generation might compel you to aspire to become some kind of influencer or famous person. You may be putting all your hopes and dreams in getting into a prestigious college or landing a lucrative job in the future.

Or perhaps, like me, the experience of seeing your parents work so hard and sacrifice for you drives your ambition.

I've been a youth pastor in a large Asian American church for a long time, and I'm a father to three children who are seeking to fulfill their future dreams following college graduation. I empathize with the Asian American ethos—especially that of teenagers and young adults—of wanting to get into a good college, to make good money, or (even just more generally) of fulfilling one's ambitions. But I've lost count of how many times over the years, during college decision season, parents at my church have asked me, "How many students from the youth group got into an Ivy League school?" When I hear this question, I want to remind parents and their teenagers that getting into Ivy League schools does not define them. Neither do good grades, nor an exemplary resume, nor material wealth.

When you feel the weight of all those expectations bearing down on you, I want you to remember the good news of the gospel. When I was feeling so inadequate that I didn't come home from college for two years, what I needed was a reminder that because of God's grace in Jesus, I was God's masterpiece.

You no longer need to define yourself by what you have achieved or how well you are performing. Instead, I pray you will find your hope and worth in the truth that Jesus loves you. God has created you in Christ Jesus, and he will lead you into a calling and purpose greater than anything you could strive to attain for yourself.

Devotional Questions

Read Ephesians 2:1–10.

1. How does Paul describe our past condition before Jesus rescued us? What has Jesus's performance—his perfect life, his death, and his resurrection—secured for our present and our future?
2. The author described the different ways he sought to prove himself through achievement or having a successful life. Where do you feel these pressures to perform in your own life?
3. Spend time thanking God today for the "good works which [he] prepared . . . for [you] to do." How could knowing that God has these good plans for you help you to rest in Jesus's work?

Honor-shame worldview (noun): The primary way that Eastern cultures see the world. Honor is given to people who act in line with their community; anyone who fails to live up to those expectations has shame placed upon them. Positively, this worldview can curb bad behavior by dissuading those who bring dishonor to the community. Negatively, it can leave us struggling with feelings of unworthiness.

What this means for you: The gospel is good news for you because your identity and worth are no longer dependent on doing all the right things. You are now secure in what Christ has done for you. Through the shame of the cross, Jesus took away our shame. As a sinful human being, you will often sin. But God will never shame you. As a Christian, you have the gift of the Holy Spirit, the ultimate sign of honor that we belong to God (Romans 5:5).

Chapter 2

Unworthiness and the God Who Saves

by Connie Leung Nelson

My family emigrated from Hong Kong to Canada in the early 1990s, when I was six years old. The first year was the hardest, when I didn't speak a word of English. The language gap made my "otherness" impossible to hide, and I quickly understood that I was different from the kids at school.

But I was different from the kids at our Chinese church too. Most of the families there had been in Canada long enough to feel established, and they navigated Canadian culture with ease. Unlike them, our family was marked by our "new immigrant" status: fresh-off-the-boat-level poor. I never dreamed of comparing myself to the kids at school who went to Disneyland during spring break and got Nintendos for Christmas. But the sting hit differently when I heard the other church families chat about where to go for lunch every Sunday after service, while we always went straight home ("There's food at home!").

My parents loved me the best they could. Their love was expressed to my sister and me not in words or hugs, but in an unwavering commitment to our health and education. Instead of "How was your day?," we heard, faithfully, "**飲湯啦** (It's soup time)!" I understand now that what my parents gave us was nothing short of lavish in comparison to the scarcity of their own upbringing.

Still, it was difficult to see or hear their love communicated in ways that were so different from how other kids experienced love from their parents. I knew, with absolute certainty, that my parents loved me, but I always wondered whether I was enough for them. And so, the poorness I felt in comparison to my peers extended to the poverty I felt in affection and affirmation at home. Even though I was so aware of all the ways my parents painstakingly provided for me, I yearned to be the object of their affection. In the deepest part of my heart, I wanted to be affirmed as someone's special person.

By the time I got to high school, I discovered a treasure trove of affirmation available to me—affirmation that tasted even better than the plate of peeled and sliced fruit my mom delivered to my room every night. That bounty was the love of my friends and the thrill of validation from my accomplishments. With each A in school or advancement in extracurriculars, each Friday night spent with friends, and every bit of attention I received from boys, I felt needed and wanted. Even serving at church became another notch on my "I'm worthy" belt.

But life didn't always deliver the results I thought I deserved. I compared myself to my peers, and there was always reason to be jealous. It didn't help that sometimes I worked hard and the results were disappointing. Other times, I was lazy but scored at the top of my class. Allowing my circumstances and accolades to dictate my value, I flip-flopped between arrogance for my accomplishments and shame for whatever fresh failure I encountered. All the while, a nagging fear remained that someday I would be exposed as a fraud, an impostor. Everything good I had was a mistake, and everything bad was what I deserved. If I failed to earn my value as a human being, the only names I could ever secure for myself would be the ones I dreaded most: Deficient. Unworthy. A disappointment.

But what about God? What does he call me?

The Jesus I Wish I Knew

God, my Creator and Maker who holds all design and ownership rights to my whole person, is the only one who can truly define who I am (Isaiah 64:8). God doesn't hold us to any standard of our own making. The sobering news is, he holds us to his standard, and his standard is nothing less than sinless perfection—the very righteousness (right standing) of Jesus Christ.

Jesus had many dazzling accomplishments while on earth. He healed the sick, controlled the weather, and even raised the dead to life. But it was his perfect love for God his Father, expressed in his sinless, completely righteous life, that was the most amazing.

God's standard has nothing to do with "breaking the ceiling" of our human limitations, reaching our fullest earning potential, or attaining the highest level of prestige. Not becoming a doctor is not a sin. (I repeat: not becoming a doctor is *not* a sin!) Getting a bad grade on a test is not a sin. Not getting into the program you wanted is not a sin. None of these makes us unworthy.

No, what truly reveals our unworthiness is something a lot more inherent to our human nature than grades: our sinful hearts.

A sinful heart is discontent and jealous (James 3:14–16). It is lazy, a bad steward of the gifts given to us (Matthew 25:14–30). It is ungrateful and unforgiving, prideful and arrogant; it says, "I don't need anyone or anything" (2 Timothy 3:1–5). A sinful heart is disbelieving toward God (Hebrews 3:12). Guilty of all these and more, I sought to be my own god by trying to define my own worth, using a measuring stick that I had no right to wield (Romans 10:3).

And so, my nightmare proved true. Before God, you and I are laid bare, our sin confirming our unworthiness. We really aren't enough. And no one—from my cousin, the piano prodigy, to your friend with the full-ride scholarship, to the kid at church who wants to become a missionary—can measure up to

God's standard. Even with our best efforts, we can never reach the mark. We've all sinned and fallen short of the glory of God (Romans 3:23). Left to ourselves, we are under the threat of God's judgment and wrath.

But then, there is Jesus.

Jesus, the completely righteous and worthiest One, has immeasurable value as the Son of God. He stood between us, sinners doomed in our trespasses, and the wrath of God. He willingly stepped into the line of fire, took the hit, his body broken, and hung on the cross. He was crushed so that we could live.

The Jesus I Want You to Know

Jesus has always known your every sin. He knows that you are unable to avert God's wrath with your achievements, but that you still try. He knows that you fail to love God above all else.

But none of that changes the fact that he loves you.

He didn't wait until you and I got it together, until we understood the correct theology, until we started to show some progress, before giving his life to save us (Romans 5:8). In his death on the cross, not only did Jesus secure for you and me unmerited justification (the "on paper" status of being cleared of all our sins, Romans 5:9), but he also secured for us adoption as children of his Father (Galatians 4:5). For those of us who believe in Jesus's life, death, and resurrection as our only lifeline (Ephesians 2:8), God has given us a new identity as his very own sons and daughters (John 1:12).

My dear friend, you are loved with a love that you neither earned nor can ever be worthy of. You are loved with a love that only Jesus could ever deserve.

Are you worthy? Am I worthy?
Of having and being everything we possess and are,
in Christ?
Of Christ himself?
No, never—not ever.
But are we of great worth, of great value?

Proven through our Rescuer, Jesus, who went to the cross
 to save us,
because of the grace freely given to us,
and as sure as his immovable love for us.
We delight in Jesus, our treasure. And as God calls us
 his very own,
he delights in us too.
(Connie Leung Nelson)

Devotional Questions

Read Romans 5:6–9.

1. What has God done for us by sending his Son, Jesus, according to Romans 5:6–9?
2. The author described many different ways in which she felt unworthy in her relationships and achievements. Are there parts of your life in which you feel unworthy?
3. How could knowing that Jesus died to give you his own righteousness in place of your sin change the way you think about yourself?

Righteousness (noun): The state of being perfectly acceptable to God in every way. Through Christ, sinners are counted as righteous before God. Another way to say it is: in Christ, you are enough.

What this means for you: Through faith in Jesus, you are counted righteous before the God of the universe. You no longer have to try to prove yourself to him or others.

Chapter 3

Weakness and the God of Strength

by Ashley Kim

In my junior year of high school, I began to feel guilty about eating. *I wish I could just stop myself*, I journaled. I was tired of feeling dissatisfied with my body, certain that if I could just exercise a little self-control to lose a little weight, I would finally achieve the elusive perfect body that I longed for.

Yet after only a few weeks of ruthless restriction, I found myself trapped in a full-blown eating disorder. For the rest of my family, seeing me cut out foods that I once found delight in eating signaled a drastic and concerning change. Meals became points of conflict as I told my mom over and over that my preferences had merely changed, that I wanted less rice, that I was already full—paper-thin lies that only barely hid my eating disorder. My family could see that something was wrong, but as I starved myself, I felt that my life was finally going to be right.

Insecurities about my body and my appearance had been mounting for years. As I became more self-conscious of my figure and of how the world would perceive me, I became increasingly convinced that if I could just be thinner, I would look more like the girls on my Instagram feed who seemed to have such effortlessly beautiful lives. I hated the self-loathing that accompanied every comparison, and I wanted to do something about it.

As a driven student, I had learned that hard work and delayed gratification were the ingredients of academic success. Why should losing weight be any different? So I set goals, made a plan, and committed. At the time, I believed that I was taking control of my own life, mastering myself, and becoming disciplined. I would make myself the person I wanted to be.

And in fact, as I set and obeyed strict food rules for myself, I did feel like I was in control. The body—and hence, the life—I always wanted was finally within reach. I found a sense of satisfaction in denying myself the pleasure of eating. I compared my eating habits to others' and congratulated myself for staying away from "bad" foods more successfully. Each time I turned down food or chose not to eat, I saw myself as a model of self-control and discipline.

Yet as I restricted more and more food, I became increasingly controlled by fear. I was plagued by the constant, irrational worry that eating *this*—whether a slice of cake, an Oreo, or a banana—would ruin my plans and end in failure. These fears were inescapable. Even when I began to face the fact that starving myself would endanger my health, I was more afraid of gaining weight than of even dying. I was certain that renouncing my eating disorder would mean giving up the one chance I had of becoming beautiful and happy. Despite barreling down a path of self-destruction, I didn't want to recover, and I didn't know how to make myself want something I feared.

Although I prided myself on my self-control, discipline, and independence—virtues that were supposed to be the key to success—I failed miserably at rescuing myself from my obsession with losing weight. The more I tried to control my eating habits, the more my eating habits controlled me. I couldn't stop.

In the midst of this shame, fear, and despair, I somehow found the courage to pray. I wasn't brave enough to ask the Lord to save me from my eating disorder. I was afraid that he would answer my prayer and take away the idol that had given me a sense of control. I was too afraid to ask the Lord for recovery.

But in desperation and trembling, I asked him to make me want recovery—to make me want to be free.

The Jesus I Wish I Knew

The Lord proved his faithfulness to be the God who "is near to the brokenhearted and saves the crushed in spirit" (Psalm 34:18). The Jesus I came to know—the Jesus of the Bible—did not ask me to just try harder or to figure out how to fix myself. All he asked of me was that I come to him in honest confession of my sin, trusting his power to save, not my own.

In my eating disorder, I believed that my success and happiness depended on my ability to say no to food. I thought I would be happy if only I could be strong enough to master the needs of my body. My biggest problem in life was that I was too weak to resist my hunger. I would be saved by my own strength; I would be my own savior. Yet my false version of self-control and self-denial led only to despair and hopelessness. Controlling my eating did not make me any happier or stronger.

As I came to Jesus in my brokenness, I saw just how sinful my desire to control my own life really was. Restricting my eating in an effort to be thin had made me the opposite of strong. I was utterly weak, unable to rescue myself from a destructive path. And in the face of this weakness, my self-control and discipline failed. My weakness could only ever be overcome by a Savior far stronger than me—the Savior we find in Christ, for "while we were still weak, at the right time Christ died for the ungodly" (Romans 5:6).

Yes, I was far weaker than I had ever thought possible. Such a realization was frightening. But I found ever sweeter depths of grace in Jesus, who had taken my sin and weakness on himself in his death and given me his complete righteousness. My only hope for healing was to forsake all hope in my own strength and to cast myself on him.

It was in my weakness, at my lowest point, that the Lord showed me his overflowing, undeserved grace. He answered my desperate prayer slowly but surely, giving me courage to confess my struggle to my mom, conviction of the sinfulness of my ways, and the desire to surrender my life and my body to his care. I began to find hope in his promises to sanctify and joy in his good design for food. While recovery was a long battle, God used it to grow my trust in his provision, kindness, and gentle strength.

The Jesus I Want You to Know

You may be tempted to believe that you were made to succeed on your own strength. The lie goes something like this: *if you don't have the looks, reputation, and self-esteem that you want, you're not trying hard enough.* Believing this led me away from Jesus and into the hopeless despair of my own sinfulness. But we were not made to be strong on our own. Jesus calls us to depend on his strength—and on one another. One of the best ways we recognize our neediness is by asking for help from someone such as a parent, a pastor, or a trained counselor.

Hear what Jesus said to the apostle Paul—and what he says to you and to me in our weakness: "My grace is sufficient for you, for my power is made perfect in weakness" (2 Corinthians 12:9). Do you feel weak, vulnerable, and insufficient? Do you see yourself continually failing as you compare yourself to others? I have good news for you: the Jesus I know is the friend of sinners. He is the kind of Savior who delights to deliver the weak and unsteady, the hopeless and despairing, the ashamed and, yes, the sinful.

Even now, Jesus calls to all who will listen, "Come to me, all who labor and are heavy laden, and I will give you rest. Take my yoke upon you, and learn from me, for I am gentle and lowly in heart, and you will find rest for your souls. For my yoke is easy, and my burden is light" (Matthew 11:28–30).

Devotional Questions

Read 2 Corinthians 12:6–10.

1. According to 2 Corinthians 12, what is Paul's attitude toward weakness?
2. The author described her struggle with an eating disorder, showing how it revealed her inability to save herself from physical distress. Think about some areas in your own life in which you're trying to exert control or succeed in your own strength. Take some time in prayer to give each one to God.
3. On the cross, Jesus turned what looked like weakness into strength as he conquered sin and death forever. Believing this, can you say with Paul "I am content with weaknesses, insults, hardships, persecutions, and calamities?" Ask God to help you see how he is making you strong in your weakness.

The gospel (noun): The good news of God's grace and redemption for sinners through the life, death, and resurrection of Jesus Christ. It is the primary message of the Bible and of Christianity.

What this means for you: When you trust the gospel, you can live freely before a God who delights in you. Because of Jesus, there is nothing you could do (and nothing you could fail to do) that will make God love you any less.

Chapter 4
Church Hurt and the Good Shepherd
by Justin Wong

Church has always been part of my life. My dad was the pastor and my mom played piano. Growing up, I felt like we lived at the church building. Even if we were too sick to go to school, we went to church. On summer break, my sister and I spent all week there with my dad. After the service on Sundays, my dad would send us off to make sure all the lights were turned off and the doors were locked.

There were always church people at our house too. My parents frequently had international students from Hong Kong over for meals, fellowship, and Bible studies. I learned that many of them could not afford to fly home for holidays, so instead they spent time with us. I observed how much these students loved our family, and how much my mom and dad loved them.

Growing up, I knew we were responsible for the church. I thought I understood how the family of God worked—until I didn't understand at all.

One day when I was in high school, our family heard a message on the answering machine that shocked us: "This message is for Pastor Wong. I don't know why you're still at this church. You're a FOB (fresh off the boat) and we can't understand anything you're preaching. You don't understand this culture and what our needs are. You really should quit and move away from this church. Bye."

We stood there in disbelief. I tried to replay the message, but my dad reached out with ninja-like reflexes and clicked the "delete" button. He looked at all of us and said, "Let's not worry about what they say. We know what God wants us to do. God will take care of it."

I couldn't understand what had just happened. How could someone from the church leave that message? And to a pastor? As I replayed the message in my mind, I knew exactly whose voice I heard on the answering machine. It was the same voice I heard the following Sunday as someone shook my hand, smiled, and said, "Hey, it's great to see you in the house of the Lord today!" I couldn't help but think, *Hey, it's a great day to punch you in the eye right now!*

The voicemails continued to come week after week, from multiple people in the church. And week after week I saw my dad delete each message. I was beyond angry. I was angry at those people, and I was beginning to resent God for doing this to my dad. *Lord, how can you allow these people to bite their pastor in the back and let them get away with it?*

I loved God and I loved his Son, Jesus. But if I was honest, I hated his people. I mean, I truly *hated* them. How could our church members be so mean, so rude, and so racist to someone who was shepherding them? They didn't see how much time my dad spent cleaning up after them. They didn't see how many hours he poured into preparing his sermons. They didn't know all the language lessons he was taking to improve his English.

Rage and bitterness from those experiences shaped much of my teenage years at church. I was frustrated with my dad for not fighting back. I was disappointed with God for not protecting our family. I couldn't worship (or didn't want to worship) and instead, just stood there cursing everyone around me in my heart.

My despondent glares toward church people became my form of judgment. Although there were only a few members that attacked our family, I turned my distrust and hurt against the whole congregation. I couldn't understand how there was so much sin among those who claimed to be Christians.

The Jesus I Wish I Knew

God used my dad to show me the heart of the gospel, to show me who Christ is.

When Jesus was reviled, he did not abuse in return. When Jesus was slapped, he didn't slap back. My dad took his cues from his Lord. At the time, I thought it was because he was weak or just being "too Chinese." I thought he didn't want to lose honor by fighting back. But I came to see that his response wasn't about shame and honor. Instead, it was his unending trust that the Lord whom he served was greater and more glorious than these light and momentary afflictions (2 Corinthians 4:17–18).

One night, I overheard my dad pray to the Lord to forgive those who spoke against him—and then he asked the Lord to soften his own heart. The Lord used this to soften my heart too. I was so consumed with pointing out the sins of others that I did not care to acknowledge the damage it was doing to me. Eventually, I had to own the way I had responded to others' sin against me.

One day after church, we went to get noodle soup for lunch. As we talked, my dad noticed that I was offering only short answers, and he asked, "兒子 (*Ah Jei*—Cantonese for "son"), what's the matter?" I told him that I was still mad at the church for how people had treated our family. It was the first time I verbalized how much I hated the church. He put his hand on my shoulder and said, "I know. But these are not your sheep or even ultimately my sheep. They are Jesus's sheep."

That was a huge moment for me. The apostle Peter teaches that Jesus is both the Shepherd of his church and our example when we suffer unjustly. He lived the perfect life, then went to the cross to pay the penalty for all the sinful things his people do (1 Peter 2:21–25). When people treated my family unjustly, I wanted vengeance. I had forgotten that these people belonged to Jesus. To hate these church people was to hate the sheep for whom Jesus laid down his life. Through my dad's example, I began to see Jesus as the Good Shepherd—both for me and for the people in our church.

Jesus, our Good Shepherd, went to the cross to save us. We're going to make a mess of things, and we're going to misrepresent him at times. He already knew this, and still he saved us and called us together.

Now, nearly twenty years later, I serve as a pastor at the very same church where I experienced so much hurt. I'm still learning that messed-up people aren't an indictment of Jesus—instead, it's those very people (myself included) whom he has come to redeem, making us into a new community.

The Jesus I Want You to Know

Maybe like me, you've been hurt by fellow Christians. Maybe it's a joke made at your expense, or that no one talked to you when you came to church for the first time (or the tenth time). Maybe it was a deep betrayal by those you trusted. Maybe it was a broken promise or watching the hypocrisy of church people outside the walls of the church building.

Remember that Jesus doesn't clean up his people before he puts them together. As long as you're in a community of sinful people, you're going to see and experience the effects of sin. It's messy and the Bible is honest about the mess.

Jesus understands church hurt more than any of us could ever imagine because he was betrayed by those he came to save. We can bring our frustration, anger, bitterness, and loneliness to him. He can handle it because he's been there too. Hebrews 4:15 says, "For we do not have a high priest who is unable to sympathize with our weaknesses, but one who in every respect has been tempted as we are, yet without sin."

This is the Jesus I want you to know: the Good Shepherd who is not afraid that his sheep will give him a bad name. The Good Shepherd who allows you to bring your hurts to him. The Good Shepherd who loves you enough to address your bitterness. Trust him with all your heart, soul, and mind, for this Good Shepherd will defend and care for his sheep.

Devotional Questions

Read 1 Peter 2:21–25.

1. How did Jesus's own trust in God the Father allow him to forgive and not "revile" those who mocked him and crucified him?
2. The author shared about some very painful experiences he and his family had in the church. Has another Christian or group of believers ever treated you unkindly?
3. How can Jesus's heart toward sinners, demonstrated on the cross, help us trust in him when others hurt us?

Good Shepherd (noun): One of the ways in which Jesus described himself is as the Good Shepherd of his people (his metaphorical sheep). As our Shepherd, he leads us and laid down his life for us. 1 Peter 2:25 and 5:4 also describe Jesus as the Shepherd of the Church, the leader of all God's people.

What this means for you: Other human beings will often disappoint us. Sadly, at times we may even experience harm within God's family. But Jesus is the Shepherd who has given his life for you. He is ultimately leading his church, even when it seems difficult to believe.

Chapter 5

Cultural Confusion and Identity in Christ

by Cory Ishida

I grew up as a teenager in the 1950s and 60s. As a typical American teenager of Japanese ancestry, I studied hard, tried to achieve straight A's, played sports with other Japanese Americans, dressed like my fellow Japanese Americans, combed my hair like fellow Japanese American guys, and had many good friends from my Japanese American church.

At the same time, as a high schooler I played ball with African Americans, participated in student government with Anglo Americans, and worked in a family business in East Los Angeles with primarily Hispanic customers.

I had convinced myself that I was the by-product of the melting pot of ethnicities called America. I got along with everyone, which made me think that my identity was multicultural. In fact, it just meant that I had friendships with everyone based on common interests—not based on a common identity.

When I was in ninth grade, I received an award at an all-school assembly. The administration secretly invited parents of the honorees to attend. After the awards were presented, they introduced our parents to everyone.

When they introduced my parents, I was embarrassed because my dad was wearing an old sport coat with a very wide tie, a remnant of post-World War II, when all of the other dads were wearing nice suits with fashionable, ultra-thin neckwear.

That same sense of shame led me to take sandwiches for lunch rather than rice balls. One time, my mom packed a bento lunch with slices of たくあん (*takuan*—pickled daikon radish), which smelled like something that had died weeks earlier. I asked her to never pack me a Japanese bento again. Peanut butter and jelly sandwiches made me feel like I fit in with my non-Japanese American friends, with whom I sat and ate my lunch.

The tension between my Japanese self and my American self was always something I felt like I could manage, but my perception of myself changed when I took a trip to Japan.

I remember standing on a corner and seeing all the Japanese people hurrying about their daily lives. It dramatically dawned on me. I was *not* Japanese. Everyone walked and talked differently. When I rode the trains, I was four inches taller than everyone else. It surprised me that I felt awkward and different. I was a foreigner in the land of my ancestors. On the other hand, I knew I couldn't eat *takuan* with my non-Japanese friends back home. At the same sobering moment, I realized I was not really a melting-pot American, but neither was I fully Japanese.

I was no longer sure who I was in terms of my identity.

The Jesus I Wish I Knew

In a moment of extreme clarity, after becoming a Christian and visiting Japan, I realized that my true identity was in Jesus. It was just as Paul wrote in Galatians 2:20, "I have been crucified with Christ; and it is no longer I who live, but Christ lives in me" (NASB).

Once my identity was secured in Jesus, that freed me to live as my whole self. I began to live life more fully as a Japanese American person whose identity was in Christ rather than ethnicity. This new understanding freed me to embrace my ethnicity. I could eat *takuan* in front of anybody. I could pastor an Asian

American church when seminaries were devaluing the role of ethnic churches.

If I had only fully known the Jesus of the Bible when I was a teenager. If my identity in him had been seared into my heart and mind, it would have saved me from a season of wandering and wondering. It would have prevented me from trying to compete academically with my Japanese American friends, compete athletically with my African American friends, compete in student government with my Anglo American friends—as though my identity was somehow interlocked with their identities. I believe that my perspective on everything would have changed and I would have navigated life in a much different manner.

I wish I had known the Jesus whose words would have given me a deeper understanding and the freedom to know and appreciate my mother and father. The first relational commandment God gave his people was to "Honor your father and your mother" (Exodus 20:12).

As an adult, after my father passed away, I took a "father journey," retracing the places my dad had lived in order to reconcile issues I had with him. As I recalled the school assembly incident, I felt ashamed for being embarrassed because of my father, who had always worked so hard. He had just an old sport coat and a wide tie because he sacrificed his own attire so that his kids could dress appropriately. Now freed from my shame around my Japanese heritage, I could see who my parents were without the distortion of embarrassment.

As a teenager, like most Japanese American young people, I obeyed my parents, but I didn't honor them as I should have. To honor someone, you have to know them. To honor someone, you appreciate them for the place of honor they have in your life. Too often, I took for granted everything my parents did for me.

Now as an old man, one of the biggest regrets in my life is not getting to know my parents better. Not hearing their stories. Not thanking them over and over again. Not celebrating their milestone occasions more fully. Not telling them how much

I loved them. I was incapable of honoring my parents as a teenager, but my faith in Christ has allowed me to revisit my past with a renewed soul and a redeemed perspective.

The Jesus I Want You to Know

Unfortunately, life has no do-overs. Life is meant to be lived once and only once (Hebrews 9:27).

I cannot go back to sit at the lunch table with my teenage friends sharing and explaining the cuisine from my bento lunch. I cannot go back and be satisfied with my SAT score even though it was lower than some of my Japanese American friends. I cannot go back and hear my father and mother regale me with their stories about life as a teenager during the Great Depression or falling in love and getting married at a World War II Japanese internment camp.[2] I cannot go back and thank them for the countless sacrifices they made to send me to college. I cannot go back and thank my father for wearing an old sport coat and a wide tie so I could dress like a teenager. I cannot go back and tell them how much I deeply loved them.

Those of you who are reading this chapter are probably the age of my grandchildren. So this would be my prayer and desire for each of you as it is for them: That you would be so much in love with Jesus. That you would be as he would want you to be and do what he desires you to do. That near the end of your lives here on earth, you will not have the regret of feeling ashamed of your parents or your heritage. Instead, I pray you will receive both as good gifts from the God whose love overflows to you in Christ.

May Jesus, who loves you and cares deeply for you, fill you with love and gratitude toward the ones who love you the most.

This is the Jesus I would want you to know.

2. Japanese internment camps were facilities in the United States from 1942–1945, where more than 120,000 Japanese Americans were forcibly relocated and incarcerated based on their ethnic background.

Devotional Questions

Read Galatians 2:20.

1. How does Paul describe the way in which Jesus has radically redefined his life and identity?
2. The author shared about feeling caught between two cultures, as though he didn't fully fit either one. Have you ever felt this as an Asian American teenager too? What are the experiences that cause you to feel "not Asian enough" or "not American enough"?
3. Jesus loves you and gave himself for you, securing for you a new identity. How could knowing this free you to celebrate the different parts of your culture and background?

Identity in Christ (noun): Understanding our true self and purpose through our relationship with and faith in Jesus. Who you are is based on who Christ is.

What this means for you: Your true worth is not found in what you do, your achievements, or other people's approval. Christ has given you a clear identity in himself: You are sinful, but you are loved and rescued in Jesus Christ. In him, you will always have a place to belong.

Chapter 6

Tragedy and a Better Friend

by Daniel Yang

I wish I had been a better friend to Chan.

We grew up in inner-city Detroit in a pretty challenging community. As Hmong Americans whose refugee immigrant parents arrived in the United States in the late 1970s and 1980s, my Hmong friends and I never felt like we fit in at school.

I was always explaining to our classmates and teachers that the Hmong were Asians but we weren't Chinese or Japanese, and our parents were refugees from Laos by way of Thailand, but "We aren't Laotian or Thai. And although Laos is next to Vietnam, our parents didn't fight the Vietnam War. They fought the war in Laos. And they weren't communists. They were the 'good guys' on the side of the Americans. And people like my dad and uncles were hired and trained by the CIA as guerrilla fighters. Both of my uncles died in the war."

Then I would pause to see if I should continue . . . sigh . . . *I'm in too deep already. Got to finish.*

"America fought a war in Laos at the same time they fought one in Vietnam. For a long time, Americans only knew about the one in Vietnam. The war in Laos was supposed to be a proxy war, but eventually it became the most bombed and shelled nation (by America) in the history of the world. It was later named the Secret War in Laos."

And that's usually when I lost whomever was listening. I wish the movie *Gran Torino* with Clint Eastwood had come out when I was growing up because I could have just referred people to it and been done with it.

Chan and I only knew each other for about a year in the seventh grade. We were barely teenagers, and we were both nerdy and awkward. But I was *really* nerdy and awkward, and tried to blend in with the urban, hip-hop style of 1990s Detroit. Google "Starter jackets" and "USED jeans brand" to get a visual. I also had long bangs with my hair parted down the middle.

Chan probably fell into the category of looking FOB: fresh off the boat. He didn't bother with the urban clothing, but he did have the parted hair. It was a signature look for Hmong kids in our era.

Most of the Hmong kids like us were just trying to survive at school. (Sometimes literally because of gang culture.) But Chan was constantly being bullied. The teachers didn't sympathize much with him. And then he had a hard home life. It was sort of a worst-case scenario for an Asian American kid growing up in Detroit.

This is the part when the story gets really sad. (Before I continue, take a meaningful pause right now and remind yourself that God loves you completely, even if you feel alone like Chan did.) Chan didn't return to school for the eighth grade. He died before school started again.

His body was found in a river sometime during the summer. It's possible that he fell or jumped off a bridge. Who really knows what went through his mind? It makes me sad to think about what he was feeling—and what he was *not* feeling.

I look back and wonder if his death was a result of the multiple layers of trauma he had experienced. There was so much complexity growing up the way we did in a community supercharged by almost every major social tension stored up in American inner-cities—racism, ethnic isolation, xenophobia,[3] poverty, broken homes, and pressure to perform.

3. Fear or hatred of strangers or foreign people and cultures.

I'm not sure if having better friends might have helped him. Maybe. But I wish more people had told Chan that he mattered. Because he did.

Decades later, I want to honor Chan and the Chans of the world. Despite the brokenness around them, and perhaps the brokenness inside of them, they matter deeply to God.

The Jesus I Wish I Knew

I was already a Christian when Chan died. And while I try not to carry too much shame or guilt for his death, I do carry a tremendous amount of sadness when I think about it. I wish I had known to ask,

> "How are you feeling?"
> "Are you feeling lonely?"
> "Do you want to talk about your anger? Your sadness?"
> "Do you want to get your mind off things?"
> Or even just, "Do you want to go do something?"

And then I wish I'd known how to listen, even if he hadn't known how to respond. I wonder if simply talking with him could have allowed him to process his feelings when he was sad or angry, so that he might have felt less lonely.

Jesus often did this for people. We see it when he engages in small talk with the Samaritan woman at the well in John 4:7. He simply asks her, "Will you give me a drink?"

Of course, Jesus was perfect. But the way John sets the scene, we get the sense that this is an awkward conversation, and Jesus was direct in getting her attention.

It was a basic question: "Will you give me a drink?"

He was in tune with the shame she was carrying. His little request for water led to a big discussion about the pain in her life. They even talked about the confusion she had when it came to her spiritual life.

In that small and seemingly impromptu conversation, she felt seen by Jesus. In fact, she went home and announced to everyone in her town, "Come, see a man who told me everything I ever did!"

As someone who felt ashamed of her life, she didn't feel judged by Jesus. He noticed her.

I don't think seventh grade me could've pulled off a John 4 conversation with anyone, at least not in the way Jesus did it. But I wonder what a conversation with Jesus would be like for a seventh grader feeling so much pressure from their social, cultural, and mental circumstances. If only everyone could hear Jesus ask,

"How are you feeling?"
"Are you feeling lonely?"
"Do you want to talk about your anger? Your sadness?"
"Do you want to get your mind off things?"
Or even just, "Do you want to go do something?"

The Jesus I Want You to Know

I wish every awkward Asian American teenager had an in-person friend to talk with this way. I never want another Asian American teenager to have to stand on a bridge feeling alone.

What matters even more to me is that you know you have this kind of friend in Jesus. He relates to the woman at the well, and he's sad thinking about Chan on the bridge. In fact, he sees you at your own well or on your own bridge.

He doesn't just see you. He's there with you.

The cross was his well and his bridge. He hung there alone, and he took all our sin and all our painful feelings on himself. And while I don't know exactly why God allows people to feel alone, I do know that Jesus understands deeply what they're feeling and what they're thinking.

And when you're sad or angry, I hope you can hear him ask you,

"How are you feeling?"
"Are you feeling lonely?"

And I hope you'll begin a conversation with him. No pressure to fix everything you're feeling. Just enough conversation to get you through the moment. He knows you perfectly, and he wants you to know him too.

That's enough, just for today.

Devotional Questions

Read John 4:1–30.

1. The Samaritan woman came to the well at an odd time of day (v. 6), likely because she was avoiding the other women in her community. How did Jesus demonstrate that he saw her and wanted to talk with her?
2. The author describes wishing he had known how to engage a lonely classmate in middle school. Who in your life needs you to reach out in friendship? Could you prayerfully make a plan to ask that person some of the questions outlined in this chapter?
3. When the Samaritan woman learned of Jesus's identity as God's Messiah (v. 26), she went from isolating herself to telling everyone about him (vv. 28–30). How could knowing Jesus make you brave in the way you relate to others?

"El Roi," the God who sees (proper noun): In the Old Testament, an Egyptian servant of Abraham and Sarah named Hagar was driven from her community and into the wilderness. God appears to her, prophesies to her, and encourages her to return. Hagar gives this name to God when he shows kindness and empathy to her. In the New Testament, it is Jesus who sees and speaks to the Samaritan woman at the well.

What this means for you: Jesus sees and knows our struggles and our pains. He invites us to share these with him through prayer, and with other believers through relationships, small groups at church, etc.

Chapter 7

Trying to Fit In and God's Acceptance

by E. L. Sherene Joseph

When I was fifteen, I arrived at my high school thirty minutes early each day, then rushed into the girls' bathroom to change my hairstyle. That's right—every day I would jump off the bus and hurry to fix my hair before the first bell.

I was in eleventh grade, and my mother forced me to wear my hair oiled in two long, tight braids with white ribbons plaited into them. My hair nearly reached my waist, and I knew my mother took great pride in it. To the South Indian community, long hair on girls was a source of pride and beauty.

But to fifteen-year-old me, it was a form of the deepest humiliation. I hated my braids and wished I could chop them off every day. My friends all had the most modern hairstyles for school. Some wore ponytails or bobs, and some even wore braids, but they were fancy French braids. None of them had a bucket of oil on their hair.

Our school catered to the education of immigrant families from all over India. I knew oiled hair was commonplace in South India, but even my South Indian friends did not have their hair oiled for school. My mother inflicted this torture on me, and I hated her for it. I looked weird and greasy. Some classmates were kind to me, but others made fun of the odd ribbons and ugly, tight plaits. It was humiliating to be in eleventh grade and not be in charge of my own hair.

So I did my best every morning to change it before class. I usually arrived back home by 3:00 p.m. and was able to redo my hair before my mother returned from work. Then, one day, I turned my key in the lock and saw my mother standing on the other side of the door. She saw that I had undone my braids and tied my hair back in a ponytail. To this day, I will never forget the way she berated me and the punishment that ensued. My mother's anger was always something I feared. She punished me for the rest of the month, and I had to wear those horrendous braids for the rest of the semester.

What hurt the most was that my mother did not understand how I felt. She didn't understand that as a teenager, all I wanted to do was to blend in. I did not want to stand out with my awful hair! Deep in my heart, I knew I could never be like the pretty and popular girls. But I hoped I could at least be normal, be accepted.

Eventually, my mother stopped doing my hair, but I still felt awkward and uncomfortable. The Indian diaspora (people who have been spread from their homeland) where we lived was more fashion-forward and modern. But my family wanted me to abide by the rules of Indian culture in India. Fashion or trying to fit in with my friends and other girls was considered silly and frivolous.

The honor-shame worldview and the performance orientation of Indian culture also pressured my parents to constantly push me out of my comfort zone to compete in every activity and program. As immigrants, their lives were all about striving and being the best. They wanted what was best for me, but sometimes it was not what I needed.

I did not feel Indian enough culturally, but I didn't feel I belonged in the diaspora culture either. So I strived. I worked hard and tried to find belonging in all the wrong places.

The Jesus I Wish I Knew

It is hard to feel like a round peg in a square hole. But that was me—a peg that just did not fit anywhere. Belonging has always been hard for me, perhaps partly because of my experience as an immigrant.

The story of Matthew (also known as Levi, the tax collector) in Luke 5 has always resonated with me. In this chapter, we see Jesus calling Matthew to follow him, and Matthew immediately becomes Jesus's disciple.

As a tax collector in first-century Palestine, Matthew was not a popular guy. Both fellow Jews and Roman citizens likely hated him, since tax collectors were known for taking a cut of the money they collected from others.

Matthew, more than likely, struggled to fit in. He was not like his Roman coworkers, and his people, the Jews, disliked him for the work he did. He was caught in between two worlds doing a job everyone hated. So when Jesus called him, Matthew did not hesitate to follow.

Matthew would have been familiar with the Old Testament and its teachings. Perhaps he didn't participate in the theft associated with tax collectors. He may have been a good, by-the-book Jewish man following all the rules and regulations, but he likely did not have a relationship with the Lord.

Perhaps he was spiritually hungry and waiting for something to happen in his life. Jesus sought him out, drew him, and called him to follow. Matthew did not need to do anything to fit in with Jesus and the other disciples. Jesus knew Matthew and understood him.

Jesus invited Matthew over for a meal, which included other tax collectors. There was something beautiful about how Jesus invited him and gave him a place to belong. Matthew would be his disciple and would go on to write one of the Gospel accounts in the Bible.

He left behind an occupation which was little esteemed and went on to be a witness for many others like himself. Jesus saw Matthew, invited him into friendship, and gave him a place to belong.

I wish I had understood all this as a teenager trying to fit in. Had I known then that Jesus accepted and loved me for who

I was, I might not have worried as much about what others thought of me. I wish I had known to find my self-worth in him instead of seeking it in other people. If I had known Jesus did not expect me to live up to a standard, I might have even found freedom in the cultural expectations of my family and community. Because I wasn't aware of his grace and acceptance, I was a prisoner of cultural norms.

It took years for me to realize that I did not have to prove myself to Jesus. He understood the insecure, confused high school girl with the oiled braids. Like Matthew, I could find true friendship in him. He was not looking for me to prove my worth in order to be accepted. The truth of the gospel and the sacrifice of Christ on the cross reminds me that I belong to him.

The Jesus I Want You to Know

Perhaps like me, you question your identity, purpose, and belonging. When you struggle to fit in, remember that Jesus, too, was considered an outcast. People found him odd.

As the son of a carpenter, Jesus was raised in a human family, but as the Son of God, he obeyed his heavenly Father's calling. He performed miracles, spoke out against the misguided leaders of his day, and ultimately went to the cross to die. Because Jesus obeyed God the Father, he didn't conform to those around him or try to fit in. He was a straight line in a crooked world.

Out of his deep, abiding love for you, God sent Jesus to die on the cross to rescue you. Just as Jesus rescued Matthew from his old life of sin and deception, Jesus died to give you new life in him too. Your culture and ethnicity are important pieces of whom God has made you to be. But belonging to him is more important still.

Sometimes in our lives, we will feel like we are odd pegs who don't fit anywhere. But rest assured, God always has good plans for those who don't feel they fit. Just look at Matthew, whom God used to write a Gospel account. Look at Jesus, our Rescuer and our example. This reality calls for us to surrender to him, but there are many blessings to being the odd peg. Your desire to belong will be found in him. When you go through seasons of struggle, remember that Jesus too, was treated like an outcast and people found him odd. The son of a simple carpenter did miracles and was a rebel during his time. But he knew his Father had called him for a greater purpose.

In Christ, you belong. In him, you have full acceptance. You are never alone when you trust in Jesus.

Devotional Questions

Read Luke 5:27–32.

1. What does it say about Jesus that he ate with sinners and outcasts? How could this change the way you relate to him?
2. The author shared about her struggle to find acceptance. Have you ever tried to change something about yourself in order to fit in?
3. Take a few moments to write down some situations in which you are worried about fitting in or gaining acceptance from other people. How could it help you to remember that God has already accepted you based on what Jesus has done?

Approval (noun): The belief that someone or something is good or acceptable.

What this means for you: You no longer have to tire yourself out seeking God's acceptance. Because of Christ's finished work on the cross, you already have the full approval of God himself—forever. He loves you. He delights in you. In Christ, you are enough.

Chapter 8
Breaking the Rules and the God Who Forgives
by Terrence Shay

I don't remember whose room I was in when we crossed the curfew boundary. I don't have a clue what time it was when we got busted.

"What are you doing here?! It's after curfew. Get back to your room. You're in trouble!"

Church retreats were the highlights of my summer as a teenager. In the pre-social media era, this was the prime opportunity to hang out, have fun, and make meaningful memories with friends.

The team patrolling the dorm was a group of well-meaning young adults commissioned by our pastor to keep us safe. We never expected they would roam dimly lit hallways and knock on doors to check for compliance. In the days before cell phones, there was no peer warning system to alert us. As soon as the knock came on our door, the party was over and the group scattered to our assigned rooms as quickly as we could.

Once I was snug under my blanket, my heart was filled with fear and shame as I imagined word getting out. I was a student leader, supposed to set an example for others to follow. *What will people say? How will they respond when I lead worship, read Scripture, and pray in front of everyone?*

Later that week, my pastor called me to his office and handed down a consequence I never could have expected. A group of us had been invited to lead a retreat for another church later that summer. This was a unique opportunity to serve with new friends, just as we were growing together in camaraderie and chemistry. I was genuinely excited and had been practicing every day to be competent for my role as worship leader. It was the first time that a group from our church was being sent to partner with another, and I was glad to step up to a greater level of responsibility.

But now my pastor informed me that, as a consequence for breaking curfew, I was no longer allowed to serve at this retreat. In fact, I couldn't even attend. Everything went haywire in my heart. I was discouraged, disillusioned, and super disappointed. Not only was he taking something away that was my offering to the Lord, but the punishment felt over-the-top. For weeks, I railed against the Lord and against my leaders at church:

This is so wrong!

The punishment doesn't fit the crime!

Why is this happening when I'm just trying to serve the church?!

As a teenager, I knew that I was far from perfect. I had plenty to learn about following Christ and growing into a mature leader. Still, my desire was to serve God and others. I felt misunderstood and unfairly judged by the leaders I had hoped to labor alongside. I felt like a bad Christian for letting my leaders down, and at the same time, I felt wrongfully typecast as a troublemaker, which was not me at all!

No one pulled me aside to ask me *why* I wasn't in my room. No one followed up to see how I was feeling inside. The process seemed overly simplistic. I longed for those in leadership to see how much I loved the church, how much I wanted to be good and godly.

Jesus already had my heart, but that summer, I needed him to resuscitate a broken one.

The Jesus I Wish I Knew

I struggled with two realities of the retreat punishment: On the one hand, I had broken a rule and deserved to be disciplined. On the other hand, I felt that my pastor and those young adult leaders weren't interested in my heart. Couldn't they see that I wanted to hang out with my friends, to grow in Christian community, and to serve God's people? The punishment for sneaking out seemed overly harsh. But as a good Asian American church kid, I simply apologized—and then kept quiet while overflowing with FOMO as everyone prepared to serve at the next retreat.

I wish that my leaders could have seen beyond the external details of the retreat sneak-out to the turmoil that was happening in my heart.

In Psalm 51, we read in great detail of the tumultuous storm in King David's soul as he confesses his sin and cries out to God for deliverance. David had sinned egregiously by committing adultery and murder. Even so, he trusts in God's kindness to forgive as he shares his failures vulnerably with the Lord. We read in David's prayer how he places his hope for restoration in God's power to discern the thoughts and intentions of the heart.

"The sacrifices of God are a broken spirit; a broken and contrite heart, O God, you will not despise" (Psalm 51:17).

Throughout the New Testament, we read stories of how Jesus also looked at the heart. He engaged people in all their weakness and failure. Whether it was Matthew the tax collector or the Samaritan woman at the well, the thief on the cross or Peter on the beach, Jesus welcomed each one into relationship, despite fully knowing the sinful condition of each heart.

Only the Son of God—one hundred percent God and one hundred percent human—can know what we are going through while simultaneously addressing our sin. He died in our place and gives us his perfect rule-keeping through the cross. Because Jesus knows my sinful heart and its inclinations, he sees clearly my desire to please him and to grow as a leader. Because Jesus has died for every single one of my failures, I can stand confident in the fresh start he has given me. Even now, the Holy Spirit is daily changing me from the inside out to be more like my Lord and Savior.

When I got caught breaking the rules on that church retreat, I wish I had known Jesus the way I know him now. Jesus is the only human being who never broke the rules—and still he does not condemn us.

The Jesus I Want You to Know

Perhaps you have also broken a rule and you got caught. Or maybe you have said or done worse things behind closed doors, and you've even gotten away with them.

We all sin against God and others. There will be times when we will all be caught and painfully exposed. When this happens to you, remember that God knows you intimately in all your failings. He sent Jesus to die on the cross to rescue you from your sin—from all the big, scary sin like David's, down to the smallest, after-hours camp infraction. There is nothing hidden that Christ's death did not atone for. We are accepted by God because our risen Savior stood in our place for every single time we have broken the rules.

Maybe like in my situation, adults in your life have judged you unfairly. Perhaps you have been shamed publicly for doing something wrong (or not doing something right). Regardless of what people think about your behavior, never forget that God knows your shortcomings and still values genuine repentance and obedience.

Jesus is different from the other authorities in our lives. Just like them, he will sometimes discipline us. But Jesus doesn't push away or label our prayers as excuses. He simultaneously sees what's in our heart, and because he died on the cross and rose again, he is able to cover our sin in full.

God is not done with us. He sees and knows everything about us even when others stop at the surface. Jesus perfectly obeyed God so that he could die in our place for all the ways we have failed. Knowing this, we can rest in his grace.

Devotional Questions

Read Colossians 1:15–23.

1. How does Paul describe Jesus (vv. 15–20)? How does he describe our condition before Jesus saved us (v. 21)?
2. The author describes feeling caught between two realities: knowing he had broken the rules and deserved a consequence, and at the same time, experiencing a lack of understanding from his leaders. Is it usually harder for you to acknowledge your sinfulness or to remember God's grace to you in Jesus?
3. Take a moment to read Psalm 51 as your own prayer, pausing to offer the Lord your thoughts as you go.

Grace (noun): Grace is God's unmerited favor. It's the unearned gift of God's blessing and love. By grace alone we are saved, through faith.

What this means for you: Because we have sinned and fallen short of God's perfect standard, we are unworthy of God's love and generosity. But through his grace shown in the life, death, and resurrection of Jesus, we have forgiveness, relationship, and mercy from the Lord every single day.

Chapter 9
Loneliness and the God Who Is Near
by Soojin Park

As a teenager, I lived the sort of dream life that church-attending Korean American parents wanted from their children, and the kind of life that many of my peers applauded.

My good grades and commitment to extracurriculars probably should have labeled me a nerd in the cruel social landscape of high school, but I somehow navigated the politics of cliques and had a vibrant social life. I participated at church, volunteered in children's ministry, and faithfully kept Friday nights open for youth group.

I had every reason to be happy and fulfilled. I was seemingly rich in relationships and accomplishments—as rich as a teenager could be.

So why was I so lonely?

During my junior and senior years of high school, I experienced for the first time a kind of loneliness that didn't just make me sad—it made me scared. I spent each day surrounded by people, exchanging words and laughs. But every night, I found myself enveloped in a sinking feeling of being alone. I wondered why the relationships in my life didn't feel concrete or real.

I knew my family loved me, but I didn't believe they accepted me. Beneath the surface of the model Asian child was a confused and hurting teenager. I hungered for a kind of emotionally sensitive dialogue that my first-generation Korean parents didn't even know existed. I never questioned my parents' obligated care for me as their child, but I felt that as a person, I was either too much for them emotionally or not enough for them academically.

I knew my friends enjoyed my friendship and we cared for each other, but I didn't believe they knew me. I wondered if my friends would stick around if I were to show them a more raw version of me. Would they enjoy my friendship if I took off the mask of a constantly happy and fun Soojin? Most importantly, did they care to know what was actually at my core?

I knew that God is always present in all places, but I didn't believe He was actually *with* me. On the outside, I was as strong in my faith as any teenager could be. I never questioned the existence of God, I could spit out a decent explanation of John 3:16, and I made church a central part of my life. However, if you peeled away the outer layers, you would find an orphan who saw God as distant and uninvolved.

You see, as a child I had endured a horrible incident of sexual assault. Although I had no physical bruising left, my soul was permanently bruised, and I was just beginning to realize this as a teenager. Whenever I genuinely experienced God's love at youth group, I immediately went back to what had happened to me and wondered why God stood by and did nothing to save me. How could God have allowed such evil to enter my life? Maybe God was present in some sense, but I couldn't believe that he was for me.

The loneliness I felt was too deep and too painful; it left me in tears many nights wondering what was wrong with me. Was I the only one who felt this?

The Jesus I Wish I Knew

It wasn't until much later that I started to really understand and believe the gospel. I've come to realize that the gospel gives a proper response to our loneliness in two main ways.

First, the gospel shows that Jesus made a way for us to never be alone by experiencing the ultimate form of loneliness through his death. Jesus was wrongly tried and betrayed by his own people, ridiculed by his neighbors, and abandoned by his closest friends. All of this pales in comparison, though, to the agony he felt as he hung on the cross all alone, crying out, "Why have you forsaken me?" to his Father, with whom he shared a perfect love. He endured abandonment in the truest sense by everyone around him as he alone carried the weight of sin on his shoulders. He faced the wrath of God alone so that we would not have to endure such loneliness.

Jesus's sacrifice made it possible for us to know with certainty that we are never alone. God the Son, who broke the barrier between man and God, calls us his friends and sympathizes with us when we experience pain and loneliness (John 15:15). God the Father sent his one and only Son to die so we could be sons and daughters of the living God. We have been adopted by a Father whose love has no boundaries and who never abandons us (Ephesians 1:5, Romans 8:15). God the Spirit dwells inside of us. No matter how much the experiences of our broken lives may cloud our emotions, what is undeniably true is that God is with us every single moment of our lives (Romans 8:11). And as adopted children of God, we are given a multitude of siblings. We are never truly alone, for we are always united to other believers, who are called to love us, care for our needs, and to do the work of Christ together with us.

Second, the gospel reminds us that God's work is still being done and has yet to be completed. Jesus will come back to finish his good work—but until then, we live in the in-between, where we still deal with sin. This means that despite the fact that God and his people are with us, we will still have moments and seasons in this life when we feel alone. Because of sin, our relationships with each other will be faulty, our church family will fail us, and we'll always seek more fulfillment from human relationships than we should. Because of sin, we'll wrestle with days and even seasons where it truly does feel as if God is not with us. Perhaps until our physical bodies are present with God in the new heavens and earth, our fickle hearts will always question if God is really with us. However, this should be a source of comfort—loneliness is a normal experience of life in this broken world. You are not alone in your struggle with loneliness. You're not extra-broken because you are in a season of loneliness.

Jesus's soon-to-be completed work also gives us hope by reminding us that experiencing pain in this life does not mean that you have been abandoned by God. If we allow our suffering to lead us to doubt God's love and protection, we'll end up in a cycle of despair. Had I known the full gospel in high school, I would not have seen God as distant and uninvolved because he allowed me to be hurt. Instead, I might have been able to see that God was deeply moved by my pain, present with me in my suffering, and that he hated the sin committed against me. In fact, he hated it so much that he sent his Son to die so that sin could be destroyed once and for all.

The Jesus I Want You to Know

While we can't always understand why things happen, the gospel helps us see God's nearness clearly. Far from leaving us alone when we suffer, God went above and beyond to make sure our suffering would end and that we could be with him forever.

Your loneliness will try to fool you into thinking you are the only one who feels this way, but remember that this is a common experience and that the gospel gives hope to us all. Like King David, who also felt deep loneliness, I hope you will go to the Lord with honesty and lay down your pain at his feet (Psalm 25:16; 142:4). He cares for you, he cares about your loneliness, and he promises that one day it will end.

Friend, if you are going through a season of loneliness and it feels too hard to bear, find rest in the fact that in Christ, *you are truly never alone*. I plead with you, don't brush this off as a cheap Christian platitude. Think deeply about the kind of loneliness that Jesus was willing to endure so that he could be with you and *for you* because he loves you.

Devotional Questions

Read Matthew 27:45–56.

1. By dying on the cross for our sin, Jesus experienced the wrath and "forsakenness" of God the Father that we all deserve. How did the onlookers at the cross interpret Jesus's words and his death?
2. The author describes the sense of loneliness she felt as a teenager, even when she appeared happy and fulfilled. Do you ever feel deeply alone, even when you're surrounded by other people?
3. How could it help you to remember that Jesus understands your loneliness because he was utterly alone on the cross?

Forsaken (adjective): As a member of the Trinity, Jesus was (and is) fully God. Because he was also fully human, he was able to take the full weight of our sin upon himself on the cross. When he did, Jesus experienced temporary abandonment from God the Father as he bore the punishment our sin deserved.

What this means for you: Because Jesus was abandoned on the cross on your behalf, God will never abandon you. When you feel alone or abandoned by others, you can be confident that God is with you. He has given you his Spirit, the third member of the Trinity, to stay with you always.

Chapter 10
Masculinity and the Son of Man
by Felix Theonugraha, PhD

I was a scrawny kid who loved sports. But I was not big enough to play the most masculine sport (or at least the one that supplied the homecoming king each year): football.

Being five feet nine, I wasn't tall enough to play basketball. In fact, right before tryouts, my dad pulled me aside and asked me, "Felix, how many Asian people do you see in the NBA?" This was before Yao Ming arrived on the scene, so the answer was "zero." My dad replied, "Remember that."

Having none of the qualities that make one "attractive" in the eyes of high school classmates, I leaned into the one thing I was good at—school (so stereotypically Asian, right?). But I soon discovered being smart makes you nerdy. My friends and I used to joke that girls don't realize the value of dating a smart guy until after college. We said things to make ourselves feel better, like "the jocks run the school now, but they'll be working for us when they grow up."

Growing up as an Asian American man in the United States is not easy. The Western ideal of masculinity is of men who are strong, fearless, and competitive. From John Wayne to John Dutton, Tom Brady to Tom Cruise, examples of desirable men often exclude Asian Americans. While in some ways things have improved (movies like *Shang-Chi and the Legend of the Ten Rings* and *Crazy Rich Asians* are attempting to normalize Asian presence in media), Asian men continue to be notably absent from mainstream rom-coms and covers of men's fitness magazines. We are seen as weak, effeminate, and undesirable—a stereotype that goes as far back as the Chinese Exclusion Act of 1882.

As if it was not enough to live under the weight of the Western masculine ideal, I found that this same social pressure about what it means to be a man crossed over into the church. When I was in high school, one particular Christian book about manhood became extremely popular. In essence, the author suggested that every man has three inherent desires—a battle to fight, an adventure to live, and a beauty to rescue. The first two characteristics run counter to the Asian values of harmony and community. The last characteristic felt impossible, given how popular culture has portrayed Asian men as less than desirable.

I did not realize how much I had internalized this message of Asian undesirability until a few years later when a friend suggested that I ask the woman who is now my wife out on a date. My first response was, "But I'm Asian! Why would she want to date me?"

At the same time, the Asian ideal of masculinity presented an equally confusing message. This ideal, rooted in Confucianism, is extremely patriarchal, holding that men are the head of the house, superior to women, more rational, more powerful, and more trustworthy. Heroes in Chinese cultures tend to be men. (The story of Mulan is a rare exception, but it captures the patriarchal dynamic well. In order to save her family, Mulan must pretend to be a man.) Yet this attitude of male superiority runs counter to the values of Western society, which emphasize equality between women and men. I would argue that male superiority also runs counter to Scripture. Genesis 1:27 makes it clear: when God created humanity, he created us male and female. Both are made in the image of God, equal in value and worth.

The standard of Asian masculinity also emphasizes stoicism—the ability to endure pain and hardship without revealing any emotions. Stoicism limits the expression of positive emotions. Many of my friends rarely heard the words "I love you" or "I am proud of you" from our immigrant fathers. Instead of affirmation, we were taught that to achieve is to meet expectations and to fail is to bring shame to the family. Experiencing these dynamics as a young man, I did not want to attain the Asian ideal of masculinity either. It felt cold and detached.

As a result, living as an Asian American man in the West caused me to feel doubly emasculated by both Western and Asian ideals. I did not quite measure up to the ideal of masculinity in either culture. It would've been easier to be White in the West or to be an Asian in the East. But to be a young Asian man growing up in the West made me feel like a fish out of water. I felt undesirable and rejected.

The Jesus I Wish I Knew

Thankfully, the good news of Jesus Christ offers a different story. As children of God, we are called to become more and more like Christ. Ephesians 4:13 encourages us to "become mature, attaining to the whole measure of the fullness of Christ" (NIV). Instead of striving to be more manly, we are called, as Eugene Peterson said, to be "fully developed within and without, fully alive like Christ" (MSG).

Philippians 2 tells us that Jesus Christ "did not consider equality with God something to be used to his own advantage; rather, he made himself nothing. . . . He humbled himself by becoming obedient to death—even death on a cross!" (vv. 6–8 NIV). Rather than merely giving us a display of physical power, Jesus displayed the fullness of his love for us through his humility and self-sacrifice.

The humility of Jesus was, in fact, a theme that occurred again and again throughout his life on earth. He was born in a lowly manger, a place where animals lived. Instead of entering Jerusalem on a horse, the ride befitting a king, Jesus entered on a donkey. Instead of fighting back against false accusations, Jesus remained silent. As the prophet Isaiah foretold, "He was oppressed and afflicted, yet he did not open his mouth" (Isaiah 53:7 NIV).

Isaiah also reminds us that Jesus "had no beauty or majesty to attract us to him, nothing in his appearance that we should desire him. He was despised and rejected by mankind, a man of suffering, and familiar with pain" (53:2–3 NIV).

These passages brought me two realizations. First, I realized that no matter how much I feel rejected because I cannot live up to either the Western or Asian ideals of masculinity, I can take comfort in knowing that Jesus was also despised and rejected. Rather, as the book of Hebrews reminds us, in Christ Jesus, "we do not have a high priest who is unable to empathize with our weaknesses, but we have one who has been tempted in every way, just as we are—yet he did not sin" (4:15 NIV). I am far from alone. Jesus Christ, the perfect Son of God, walks with me. I am far from rejected. Christ, the Son of Man, has died for me.

Second, instead of trying to live up to some cultural ideals of masculinity, I realized that there is great freedom in the call of Jesus for me to become more like him. I might not be able to play football or be emotionally stoic, but I could try to become humble like Christ. Rather than feeling defeated and discouraged at what I cannot do, I can use my effort to treat others as Christ would treat them.

Had I realized all of this while I was in high school, I would have spent less time wishing that I looked more like the pop stars whom all the girls, even the Asian girls, were swooning over. Instead, I would have focused more on developing things that matter—becoming a faithful follower of Jesus and extending the love of Jesus to everyone I encountered.

The Jesus I Want You to Know

Maybe you've wondered whether you will ever measure up to certain social norms and what that says about your future. As one who has been rescued by Christ, you are called to become like him. The call of the gospel is for us to produce the fruit of the Spirit. And instead of fighting a battle, going on an adventure, or rescuing a beauty, "the fruit of the Spirit is love, joy, peace, patience, kindness, goodness, faithfulness, gentleness, [and] self-control" (Galatians 5:22–23).

You might be insecure about your body, feeling like you're not big enough, athletic enough, or man enough. But I want you to know that producing the fruit of the Spirit does not depend on the size of your body, the culture you grow up in, or the messages you receive about masculinity. If you belong to Jesus, the Holy Spirit lives in you. He will empower you to become more and more like Jesus.

Devotional Questions

Read Galatians 5:19–26.

1. How does Paul distinguish between "the works of the flesh" and "the fruit of the Spirit" in Galatians 5:19–26?
2. The author shared some ways he didn't fit the social norms of masculinity as a young Asian American man. Whether you are a guy or a girl, have you ever struggled with the sense that you have to fit a certain mold?
3. What are some of the ways you'd like to become more like Jesus? Take a few minutes to journal these hopes as a prayer today.

Son of Man (noun): In the Old Testament book of Daniel, the prophet describes a vision of "one like a son of man" (Daniel 7:13). This coming king would one day reign over the world, and people from every nation and language would worship him. Jesus often referred to himself as "the Son of Man," showing that he is the king God had promised.

What this means for you: Because Jesus is fully God, he was able to bear our sin on the cross, taking away our shame. Because he is also fully man, he shows us what it means to be truly human. As Jesus lived and ministered in a human body, he depended on the Holy Spirit. As we follow him, we depend on the Spirit too.

Chapter 11

Multiethnicity and the Family of God

by Raymond Chang

Growing up, my parents would prevent me from taking 오이김치 (*Oh Ee Kimchi*—pickled, spicy cucumber) and steamed rice to school. Despite speaking at least two languages, they tried to conceal their accent or chose not to speak because they didn't speak English perfectly. Perhaps because of these things, I internalized a perpetual inferior label to whatever was Korean or Asian American.

I projected this internalized sense of shame onto the Korean American church in which I grew up, feeling that it was a second-class haven for me and others like me. Subconsciously, it was the *Korean American* or *Asian American* modifiers that made me assign a lower value to the churches to which I belonged.

Still, I know the church had a significant role in my surrendering to Jesus. As an eighth-generation Christian, my faith was passed down from generations past, as well as through the local church.

It was in the Korean American immigrant church that I learned what it meant to be a Christian and what it meant to be a Korean American. Through the church, I learned how to pray, to love God's Word, and to serve God by serving others. I also learned what it meant to support fellow Christians and to make sacrifices for the broader community.

My parents were drawn to church because of their faith in God, but also because it was the one community to which they could experience meaningful belonging. It was the only place where their minority language was normalized, the only place where their struggles were commonly understood. Even though they were small business owners, it was the only place where they weren't treated as second class.

My parents and others like them huddled in these churches because they needed to as a means of survival. When you look at the history of Asian Americans in the United States, the discrimination and racism we have experienced has converged around the same common themes. Many have experienced exploited labor, including an often-ignored working class as well as an intellectual class that continues to hit the bamboo ceiling.[4] As Asian Americans, we often experience orientalism[5] and being treated like perpetual foreigners. We also carry the burdensome weight of the model minority label (unless we are viewed as the underclass minority as many Brown Asians experience).

I have many Asian American friends who grew up thinking they were White (because they knew they weren't Black, and they thought the only other option was to be White), despite growing up in an Asian American church. It was as if they didn't see themselves because of a racialized lens imposed on them—a lens that made them invisible to themselves.

It didn't help that there were almost no conversations taking place in the home or at church about what it meant to be an Asian American Christian—let alone a Korean American Christian. One important factor contributing to this issue was that many of our senior pastors and youth pastors were trained in White evangelical seminaries being taught what it meant to do theology, ministry, and discipleship from a White perspective and cultural frameworks.

Most of our parents have never talked with us about these dynamics because they often don't know how to articulate their

4. Barriers that limit Asians advancement in professional settings.
5. Stereotyping Asian cultures as exotic and backward.

experience as Asian Americans, or they struggle to acknowledge it. If that's not complicated enough, a lot of our parents also unintentionally contributed to the erasure of our cultural heritage because they wanted us to gain acceptance by assimilating. So while they wanted us to know what it meant to be Korean, they also wanted us to be selectively Korean. Some even prohibited their children from learning and speaking Korean. They knew through experience and intuition that being Asian in the United States was a disadvantage.

It almost felt like the Korean American immigrant church wanted us to be Korean, but Jesus, through his Asian American conduits, wanted us to be White. In many ways, I think we were unintentionally told that our Asian American identity and culture was a hurdle to our Christian faith. While our ethnic and cultural identities were deemed important to preserve, they were also communicated as obstacles to overcome.

The Jesus I Wish I Knew

Growing up, I wish I had known that Jesus gave significance to the many parts making up one body and emphasized the importance of giving greater honor to the members that received less honor (1 Corinthians 12). I wish I had known how committed Jesus was to justice and wholeness—so much that he willingly picked up a cross to his own demise and demonstrated a sacrificial commitment to making all things new (Revelation 21:5). He did this not only so I would receive eternal life (1 Peter 2:24), but also so that all that is wrong with the world would be made right (Colossians 1:20).

I wish that as a teenager, I had known that Jesus delighted in the redemptive journey of my ancestors. I wish I had realized how much he loved me and all my experiences as a Korean American. My family came to faith eight generations ago. This will make my daughter a ninth-generation Christian. God has been the animating force of our family for hundreds of years, through colonial occupation, wars, the tearing apart of a people into North and South, and other major events in our history.

God is the reason my parents have organized their entire lives to preach God's Word and pray for people as they do ministry together. God was with them as my dad journeyed through the Middle East and my mom sojourned through Argentina to make their way to the United States. God is the reason my grandmother (my dad's mother) spent all her days doing visitations and praying all throughout the night on her worn-down knees with her tattered Bible open above her head. God is the reason my grandfather (my mother's dad) asked us to purchase new hymnals for the church on his deathbed.

I only wish I knew the other stories that I have never heard and won't be able to hear until I enter the unhindered presence of God. Jesus has been part of our family's story—even the details that aren't recorded anywhere beyond his knowledge. And God has been working across time and place in other families, among other peoples throughout the world. In the Bible, we see how God loves the nations—so much so, Jesus came to redeem and reconcile all things to himself.

In Revelation 7:9, we see a stunning picture of people from every tribe, nation, and tongue gathered together in communal fellowship with God. God loves the different people groups, and this is a big part of the work that I love doing with the Asian American Christian Collaborative. We let fellow Asian American Christians know that God is working through them in a way that is unique to them. We also let the rest of the Church know that the perspectives, voices, and contributions of Asian American Christians are essential to the health of the body of Christ.

I wish that our church had known how to hold my Korean and Asian American identity together with my Christian faith. I wish our church could have taught my parents how to do the same. I desperately needed someone to sit me down, look into my eyes, and tell me, "God loves you, God loves the Asian American church and all its cultural distinctions, and God is working through the Asian American church to display his goodness and glory."

The Jesus I Want You to Know

Whatever your background, I hope you know you are not a mistake. I hope you know God has been working through all history and has made you uniquely you. What your family, your ancestors, and your people have gone through in the course of history, God is redeeming in and through you. He is using your specific story to contribute to the broader body of Christ. It will take some time to dig and discover, to confront and explore, and then live out all that God has deposited into you.

There is so much that you add to the Christian community as you faithfully follow Jesus through all the things that make you uniquely you. Because Jesus showed up on this earth as a Jewish man in a particular time and particular place with a unique heritage that can be traced through his genealogy, know that God wants you to show up as the Korean, Chinese, Filipino/a, Japanese, Vietnamese, Hmong, Cambodian, Indian, Pakistani, Sri Lankan, Mongolian, Laotian, Thai, Indonesian, Bhutanese, Nepali, Karen, or Chin that God has made you to be.

God loves you, God loves the Asian American church, and I hope you love her too. Whether you are aware of it or not, the Asian American church bears witness to God's faithfulness and to the power of the gospel to withstand the powers and principalities that drive division in this world (including through racism). We have much to be grateful for in the faithful witness of the Asian American church. God continues to use his people to display his glory.

Devotional Questions

Read Revelation 7:9–17.

1. According to Revelation 7:9, who are the people from "every nation, tribe, people, and language" (NIV) in John's vision?
2. The author mentions some specific ways he was taught to hide his Korean or broader Asian background. What

parts of your culture might you feel compelled to hide or change?

3. How could knowing that you belong to the body of Christ help you to embrace and celebrate your culture? How does knowing that Jesus welcomes your particular culture help you to worship him more fully in your church context?

Body of Christ, the (noun): This is the worldwide church, Christ's hands and feet on earth—you and me and our various local churches throughout history.

What this means for you: If you are a Christian, you are a member of the body of Christ. God intends for the church to be a wellspring of Jesus and the gospel in your life. Ethnic and immigrant churches are a valuable part of this unified body of Christ, bringing the gospel to the ends of the earth.

Chapter 12

Feeling Forgotten and God's Adoption

by Jonathan Holmes

To All the Kids Who Never Felt Like They Fit In

There's a saying that goes something like this
"That's like trying to put a square peg in a round hole"
I think it's meant to convey
that sometimes who we are doesn't always
fit
with
the
situations, the people, the places, the churches, the schools
we are in.

But over time the square peg
wants to fit in.
So they whittle themselves down
Smooth out their edges
They say goodbye to those pesky 90° angles
And over time they just shove themselves
Down
Down
Down

Into the round hole
Simply because it's easier to fit in

But deep, deep down inside it's not so much about fitting in,
it's about belonging.
It's about round holes opening up a bit to let
Square pegs like you find a place to live.

There's a verse that goes something like this
God sets the lonely in families
But why did he have to stick me with a family
That looks nothing like me
Like a square peg in a round hole?
(Jonathan Holmes)

Growing up as a Korean American adoptee in a White family with a very non-Asian last name, I learned quickly that there was something about me that didn't quite fit and didn't quite belong. From home to church to school, my earliest years were spent never seeing anyone who looked like me. That set up an internal struggle, which has been a part of my consciousness for as long as I can remember: wanting to be seen and fit in, but not wanting to be seen and wanting to hide.

As a student in a majority-White Christian school, that internal struggle seesawed, but what often won out was a desire to belong and be a part of the in-crowd. All of the usual ways popularity is achieved were closed off to me, however. I wasn't athletic. (I've never played an organized sport in my life. Trust me, you do not want to see me on the basketball court.) I didn't possess movie-star looks. So I played the one card in my hand I could play, and that was my academic acumen (and even that's pushing it a bit).

My sophomore year in high school, we had to read Charles Dickens's novel, *Great Expectations*, for English class. Mrs. Stover (I'm so sorry if you're reading this now!) had the class write a three-page critical review to turn in. Many of my fellow classmates abhorred Dickens's dense prose and thus did not want to complete the review. Seeing an opening, I volunteered to write my classmates' reviews for them. One afternoon, I was called to the principal's office along with two of my fellow classmates.

Our principal began reading portions of the other students' reviews and immediately I realized I had printed two of the same reviews. Cue the beads of sweat instantly dripping down my forehead. Somehow, someway, the bell rang and our principal got up to teach his class. He looked at the three of us and said, "I'll see you next period." But that never came. To this day, I don't know if he just forgot or if he chose to show mercy. Either way, I dodged a bullet.

Looking back, I ask myself what in the world possessed me to do something so reckless. I mean, Asian Americans aren't exactly known for being daredevils, right? Something deep down inside me craved the approval of my peers. My desire to belong and fit in overrode all the normal inhibitions.

In addition to being an Asian American, I'm also adopted, which is another layer of my identity. Talk about a double whammy—Asian American and adopted (not the kind of triple AAA rating you want). As an adoptee, I think I've always wanted to belong. I venture to guess most adoptees do. Despite my adoptive parents' efforts to love and care for me, questions still persisted in my mind:

Why was I adopted?
Why couldn't my father and mother keep me?
Do you really want me?
Am I a burden?
Do I cost you too much?
Do you wish you had biological children instead of me?
Do you ever have regrets about getting me?
If God really loves and cares about me, why did he allow me to be adopted?

The Jesus I Wish I Knew

I tried to stuff many of the questions associated with my adoption and cultural identity deep down inside. I knew things about God, but looking back now, I didn't *know* God personally. There is a huge difference between knowing something and knowing *someone*. Knowledge is good if you're competing on *Jeopardy*, but when you're trying to figure out who you are, what you really want is a *person*. A Person who knows you inside and out; the best and the worst things about you and still loves you to the moon and back.

As I looked for acceptance and belonging in my high school years, my heart and mind were filled with questions. During times like these, Scripture wants to cut through the noise and difficulty to assure us of something good and true. One passage I wish I had taken to heart as a high school student is the prophet Isaiah's words:

> "Can a woman forget her nursing child,
> that she should have no compassion on the son
> of her womb?
> Even these may forget,
> yet I will not forget you.
> Behold, I have engraved you on the palms of my hands;
> your walls are continually before me." (Isaiah 49:15–16)

Using a vivid illustration, Isaiah conveys a truth that needs to sink deep inside your heart. Isaiah asks the question, "Can a mom forget her baby?" The obvious answer is no, but here's the rub: Isaiah asks us to imagine for a moment that this is in fact a possibility. Isaiah goes on to say even though a mother may forget her child, God will *never* forget you. In fact, he says, God will engrave you on the palm of his hands. We are continually before him, the apple of his eyes (Deuteronomy 32:10; Psalm 17:8).

Let that sink in for a moment, because if you're reading this as an Asian American adoptee, then you might think to yourself, *Well, my mother actually did forget me. She left me. She abandoned me. She rejected me.* Trust me, friend, I know that feeling. I've said those words to myself. But know this: even in a dark and broken world where your birth mother might have forgotten you, the God of this universe has never forgotten you. Not even for a millisecond of your existence. You are the apple of his eye.

I wish I had known this in high school. I thought God was distant and uninterested in my life. Powerful? Never doubted it. Sovereign? Yep, got that. But compassionate and loving? I had a ton of doubts. However, God has always been interested and close. I just didn't realize it. The God of Isaiah is the same God who forever holds me close to his heart.

The Jesus I Want You to Know

Even on your darkest nights and dimmest days, our God sees and knows your pain. He sees you trying to fit in. He sees you lowering your gaze to avoid eye contact. He sees you shuffling to and from class trying not to be noticed. He sees the tears you cry at night, wondering why your story of adoption has unfolded the way it has.

He is a God who takes square pegs like you and me and places us into his family. In Psalm 68, David writes, "God sets the lonely in families" (NIV).

This is the best of news for people like you and me, for the square pegs of the world: God has chosen you in Christ. He has set his steadfast love on you, which can never be taken away. He has placed you in his family because of the person and work of Jesus Christ. Jesus, the One who took the punishment for our sin and the shame of our past, stands in the gap for you. He faced and lived through the abandonment of the Father in order to bring you into the family of God.

That, my friend, is better than any feeling of fitting in; it's a reality that has been accomplished through Christ for you.

Devotional Questions

Read Galatians 4:4–7.

1. How does Galatians 4 show the fulfillment of God's promise to "set the lonely in families?"
2. The author outlined a number of questions with which he has wrestled as an adoptee. Have you ever asked yourself any of these questions? Even if you're not an adoptee, have you ever felt like a square peg in a round hole?
3. Paul says that being God's child means you are also his "heir" (Galatians 4:7). How does it give you hope for the future to know that you have an inheritance with Jesus?

Spiritual adoption (noun): Being welcomed into the family of God through the Son, Jesus Christ, and receiving all the privileges of rightful children.

What this means for you: Although we have all rebelled against God in sin, he extends forgiveness to us through Jesus Christ. When we put our trust and faith in him, we become a part of God's new family, with all of the benefits of being his child granted to us through Jesus.

Afterword

by Kevin Yi

Thank you for reading this book. It has been a labor of love to gather these stories and these authors together, asking them to bare their souls so that you would be edified and renewed. It's not often that we as Asian Americans are invited to tell our unique stories, share our particular pains, and write about how Christ has graciously redeemed them for us. We hope that in these chapters, you saw people who have struggled as you do, and offer a very real hope to you in the person and work of Jesus Christ.

Before we close out this book, I want to leave you with one more encouragement from the Scriptures.

Do you remember how the twelve apostles were chosen? Luke 6:12–13 tells us that Jesus went to a mountain to pray, and "all night he continued in prayer to God. And when day came, he called his disciples and chose from them twelve, whom he named apostles" This is a remarkable picture: Jesus, the Son of God, prayed to God the Father about choosing the twelve apostles *all* night. Even though I grew up in the Korean immigrant church with our intense sunrise prayers, it was super-rare for me to pray about something all night. Okay, to tell you the truth, I've *never* prayed about something all night.

Clearly, Jesus was seriously focused when it came to the choosing of the apostles. But thinking a little deeper, what did

Jesus pray about all night? "Father, reveal who the disciples are to me?" Maybe. But I think Jesus was most likely fervently in prayer *for* his apostles. Romans 8:34 tells us that Jesus, right now is "interceding for us." That is, he is praying for us as he reigns in heaven.

This intentionality of Jesus is our glimpse into the extraordinary heart of God for the nations. The Son of God stayed up all night to pray for the disciples, who would minister alongside him for three years. They would eventually become the first martyrs of the church, giving their lives so that others could know and follow him. The apostle Thomas (the one who is often labeled as "doubting") would journey as far east as India, giving his life for the sake of gospel mission to Asia.

As Asian Americans, let's not forget that our gospel roots go deep: they go all the way back to the mind and heart of Christ. While so many of our stories are filled with pain and struggle, isolation and shame, know that in Christ, all of our stories will find redemption and fulfillment.

Glossary

Approval (noun): The belief that someone or something is good or acceptable.

Body of Christ, the (noun): This is the worldwide church, Christ's hands and feet on earth—you and me and our various local churches throughout history.

Forsaken (adjective): As a member of the Trinity, Jesus was (and is) fully God. Because he was also fully human, he was able to take the full weight of our sin upon himself on the cross. When he did, Jesus experienced temporary abandonment from God the Father as he bore the punishment our sin deserved.

Good Shepherd (noun): One of the ways in which Jesus described himself was as the Good Shepherd of his people (his metaphorical sheep). As our Shepherd, he leads us and laid down his life for us. 1 Peter 2:25 and 5:4 also describe Jesus as the Shepherd of the Church, the leader of all God's people.

Gospel, the (noun): The good news of God's grace and redemption for sinners through the life, death, and resurrection of Jesus Christ. It is the primary message of the Bible and of Christianity.

Grace (noun): Grace is God's unmerited favor. It's the unearned gift of God's blessing and love. By grace alone we are saved, through faith.

"El Roi," The God Who Sees (proper noun): In the Old Testament, an Egyptian servant of Abraham and Sarah named

Hagar was driven from her community and into the wilderness. God appears to her, prophesies to her, and encourages her to return. Hagar gives this name to God when he shows kindness and empathy to her. In the New Testament, it is Jesus who sees and speaks to the Samaritan woman at the well.

Honor-shame worldview (noun): The primary way that Eastern cultures see the world. Honor is given to people who act in line with their community; anyone who fails to live up to those expectations has shame placed upon them. Positively, this worldview can curb bad behavior by dissuading those who bring dishonor to the community. Negatively, it can leave us struggling with feelings of unworthiness.

Identity in Christ (noun): Understanding our true self and purpose through our relationship with and faith in Jesus. Who you are is based on who Christ is.

Righteousness (noun): The state of being perfectly acceptable to God in every way. Through Christ, sinners are counted as righteous before God. Another way to say it is: in Christ, you are enough.

Son of Man (noun): In the Old Testament book of Daniel, the prophet describes a vision of "one like a son of man" (Daniel 7:13). This coming king would one day reign over the world, and people from every nation and language would worship him. Jesus often referred to himself as "the Son of Man," showing that he is the king God had promised.

Spiritual Adoption (noun): Being welcomed into the family of God through the Son, Jesus Christ, and receiving all the privileges of rightful children.

Equipping and empowering churches and parents to faithfully disciple students toward lifelong faith in Jesus Christ.

www.rootedministry.com

Check out our: Articles, Books, Podcasts, Conference, YouTube, Curriculum, Training, Courses, and Mentorship Program